DRIVE ALIVE II

BY

Johnny Scott III

Copyright © 2024 Johnny Scott III

All Rights Reserved

ISBN: 979-8-9887355-7-1

Editing: Kelly Deltoro-White & Wandah Gibbs, Ed. D.

Cover Illustration: Stacy Wilson

Printed in the USA

WGW Publishing Inc.

621 Wellington Avenue

Rochester, NY 14619

(585) 245-0285

DEDICATION

To my mother, Dr. Margie Lovett Scott, and to my late father Johnny Scott Sr. (February 28, 1941 - November 14, 2017). You taught me many valuable lessons.

To Betty Shaw, the author of the book One Simple Text, and Liz Marks—the daughter whose story she told.

To my family: my sons Johnny, Quin, and Rhashard; my daughter, Kayla; my grandsons Kenny, and Quin; Grant; and my godmother, Shirley.

Ode to my late grandson Johnny Brynner Scott, may he rest in heaven.

To my driving school "mom," Santosh Marwaha.

Last, but not least, this book is dedicated to Harry Marwaha, founder of the ABC Driving School.

INTRODUCTION: FROM THEN TO NOW

Good driving education *matters*. A good driver is one who can keep themselves, and everyone around them, safe on the road. Often, however, people with lots of driving experience become complacent in their driving habits. They cut corners and drive distracted, endangering themselves and others without thinking, as they go about their lives. Worse, they can pass on their bad habits to new drivers who don't know their driving right from wrong. It only takes one moment for a bad habit to become a catastrophic accident. That's why it's imperative for new (and experienced) drivers to take lessons from experienced, certified instructors, like those at ABC School of Driving.

ABC's story began 47 years ago when Harnam Dass Marwaha—known to his friends as Harry—had a vision. He wanted to create a driving school committed to excellence and student success. Harry felt driving students would learn faster and drive sooner with great driving education. Truly top-notch instructors are efficient. They find problems and fix them before their students know what's happening. Harry knew that getting world-class driving education was the best way for new drivers to begin their lives and live them to the fullest. His vision became the ABC School Of Driving, in Rochester, NY.

In those early years, Harry did everything. He was the driving instructor, office secretary and class lecturer. Whatever had to be done, he did it. He took students out in cars. He taught the 5-hour pre-licensing class and the 6-hour point and insurance reduction class (a.k.a. the defensive driving class). Forty-seven years later, the ABC School of Driving is the #1 rated driver and traffic safety education training school in the greater Rochester area.

I am proud to be one of the ABC School of Driving's certified driving instructors. I've seen many changes in the 50+ years I've been administering road tests and educating drivers. New York State (NYS) driving requirements have gotten stricter, and road safety has become more important to the public.

Vehicle technology has brought GPS, cameras, and other helps/distractions into our cars. Despite how things have changed, however, a lot of things have stayed the same. A good driver is still one who can calmly observe, assess and respond to changing situations, all while obeying the laws and regulations of the road.

The road test—then to now

When I started evaluating road test examinees, circa 1968, the NY State Road Test comprised of the following tasks:

- Buckling seat belt
- Adjusting the mirrors
- Adjusting the driver's seat
- Effectively leaving the parking space
- Turning, including left turns, right turns, and intersection turns
- Dealing with stop signs
- Making a three-point turn (a.k.a. the "k-turn")
- Making a broken U-turn
- Navigating the parallel/parallel parking between two cars
- Using hand signals

One of our popular road test sites was at the corner of Syke and Maple streets. In those days, official road test results arrived in the mail about two days after the test was completed. Most examiners however, would cut the suspense by telling examinees whether they had passed or not at the end of the test. If the student passed, they would receive a temporary driver's license in the form of a yellow piece of paper. Today, we would call this a road test evaluation sheet. The actual driver's license document would arrive in the mail a few days later. It looked a lot like a NYS vehicle registration does today—with no picture and an ID number as long as a Vehicle Identification Number (VIN).

Over time, the license documents and the licensing process changed. The first NYS photo-ID drivers' licenses were created and distributed in 1986. In 1992, the state added multiple layers of imagery to the document to prevent people from making forgeries. Driver photo IDs were printed in color beginning in 1994, and in 1996 the state changed the background color on the driver's licenses to pink.

As technology advanced and law enforcement needs changed, other aspects of the license changed. The long ID number became a 9-digit "Client ID number," and the back of the license sported a magnetic stripe similar to those found on credit cards. This made it easier for law enforcement officials to verify a driver's ID upon pulling them over. All an officer had to do was swipe the driver's license in the patrol car's computer system. The driver's full history—good and bad—would then immediately appear on the officer's screen.

In 2005, the NYS Driver's License background color changed again—this time to blue. NYS drivers were also introduced to the Enhanced Driver's License for the first time. The Enhanced Drivers' Licenses got updated in 2008, with the new licenses sporting a microchip similar to those found in passports. The new license doesn't provide entry to as many countries as a traditional passport does. It did, however, make it easier for NYS drivers post-9/11 to cross the border into Canada, Mexico, and a few Caribbean countries. Airport security checkpoints, federal buildings and military bases also accept the EDL as proof of ID.

The driver's license landscape changed again October 30, 2017, when New York State began issuing drivers the Real ID License. Real ID is similar to the Enhanced Driver's license because it is acceptable proof of ID at airport security. It cannot, however, be used to cross the United States' border.

The licensing process has also changed over the years. The three-hour in-person pre-licensing class became a five-hour class. Road test examinees who took the online class no longer had to bring their print certificates to the test. Instead, their participation and proof-of-passing is automatically uploaded into the examiners' database. This makes it easy for road test examiners to verify if a test-taker has actually done the required prep work.

In today's road test world, everything is checked and cross-checked by audio. For example, examiners now record and file every road test they administer. It makes it easy to verify examinee complaints about examiners and/or their testing experience. All the examiner's supervisor has to do is pull up the audio of the exact time, date, and location of the road test to see if the complaint is valid. This keeps the license exam process transparent at every point. It also protects everyone from becoming a victim of misunderstanding and/or malice.

Safety is particularly important to road test examiners. Every road test requires examiners to sit in a car with, and be driven around by a complete stranger. They don't have any factual information about the person taking the test. All the examiners really know is that the examinee passed their pre-licensing course and has their basic paperwork filled out. This doesn't mean they have learned the necessary skills to drive safely.

In my experience, a student's ability to make left and right turns, press the accelerator, and apply the brakes does not make them a safe, competent driver. Getting into a vehicle with an incompetent driver is intensely dangerous. As a result, all examiners have experienced dangerous situations, including accidents during road tests.

Drivers' Ed with expectations

Like my dude, Harry, I've always felt that good drivers are *educated* drivers. I tell my students to get a good night's rest before coming to my driving class. Why? Because I work my driving students as hard as I work my karate students! Like karate, good driving requires attention, focus, and stamina. I constantly check in with my students to make sure they've understood the lessons I've taught them. I use a variety of checks, including homework and verbal quizzes that they must pass to go to the next level.

My colleagues and I may all have different teaching styles, but when it comes to drivers' education, we are all on the same page. Our driving lessons focus on developing good habits by practicing what we learn. We start by practicing what we preach. ABC School of

Driving instructors are always professional and content-focused. We never text or use our personal cell phones during lessons, nor do we make personal stops while students drive around town. Most of all, we pay attention to our students' needs, giving them more than their money's worth as we assess and respond to them in real time.

The effort is worth it. Our students build the skill set they need to be successful, safe drivers for LIFE. Their success is reflected in the high passing rate ABC School of Driving students have at the New York state road test. We keep our doors open to our students even after the road test is over. Our goal is keeping drivers safe. We do this by providing driving and defensive driving courses to keep drivers sharp throughout their driving life.

This book is the written version of the lessons my colleagues and I teach at ABC. It also lays out in clear lists the things most people forget to do, or think about, when taking the New York State road test. After all, being prepared is the best way to ensure a good outcome on the road and in life.

Statistics have shown that many road test-takers who fail their exam have difficulty accepting their situation. (This is one reason road test results are now issued online after 6 pm instead of immediately after the exam.) These test-takers may cry or yell, or even call their own road test before the test has concluded. Many refuse to listen to what the examiner has to say at the end, and the situation is difficult for everyone involved. Then, after all that, the same people *reschedule* their road test, hoping a different examiner will give them a different result, without understanding why they failed in the first place.

Here's the thing—a student driver can fail the road test for doing only *one thing* wrong. So, when an examinee gets a long list of mistakes with their road test results, it means that they were nowhere *near* ready to attempt their road test nor drive alone. Their failure was inevitable. This book works to prevent those failures by giving students a bird's eye view of the exam's inner workings. It reinforces the lessons given by certified driving instructors and gives students useful insight into NYS driving regulations. It helps learning drivers to get into a safe driver headspace so they can go from first turns with your instructor to acing your road test—and beyond.

Here's how the book works: Part I takes you through the challenges and expectations drivers need to meet to pass the New York State road test. Part II gets into the finer details of safe driving practices. It gives examples of potential road challenges drivers will face and important practices every driver should have.

Finally, Part III reviews some of the material and provides drivers of all levels a chance to test their knowledge and root out areas where their skills might need sharpening. By the end of this text, every driver will have what it takes to stay safe and Drive Alive.

TABLE OF CONTENTS

PART I: UNDERSTANDING THE ROAD TEST

Chapter 1	Today's Road Test	Page 2
Chapter 2	The Snow Test	Page 10
Chapter 3	Test Disqualification	Page 18

PART II: DRIVING DETAILS

Chapter 4	Leaving the Curb	Page 30
Chapter 5	Turning and Intersections	Page 34
Chapter 6	Parking, Backing & U-Turns	Page 46
Chapter 7	Vehicle Control	Page 56
Chapter 8	When Stop Means Stop	Page 80
Chapter 9	Law Enforcement on the Road	Page 88
Chapter 10	The Problem with Texting	Page 96

PART III: REVIEW AND APPLICATION

Chapter 11	Time to Think	Page 106

INSTRUCTOR REVIEWS   Page 114

PART I

UNDERSTANDING THE ROAD TEST

CHAPTER 1   TODAY'S ROAD TEST

Today's road tests aren't much different from the tests of yesteryear. The examinee arrives at the official testing site with:

- A licensed accompanying driver
- A copy of their NYS learner's permit
- A copy of their five-hour pre-licensing class certificate
- And (if using a privately owned vehicle to take the test) a copy of the vehicle's current registration.

Drivers under 18 also need to have a signed MV262 form indicating they've had a minimum of 50 hours of supervised driving practice while accompanied by a licensed adult.

After the examiner processes the examinee's paperwork, they quickly examine the vehicle being used for the test. They then get into the passenger side of the vehicle as the examinee gets into place on the driver's side. The test taker and NYS road test examiner then leave the parking space and begin the test. The accompanying driver (whether a private individual or a driving school instructor) waits outside the vehicle at the site.

At a minimum, examinees can expect to be tested on the following skills:

- Leaving the parking space
- Turning at intersections
- Left and right turns
- Stop signs
- Driving in traffic
- Steering control
- Speed control
- Parallel parking
- The three-point turn (a.k.a. the "k-" or "broken u" turn

The test's relative simplicity prompts many road test takers to feel overconfident on the day of their test. If an examiner thinks the test taker hasn't mastered one or more of the essential skills however, they can end the test immediately. Translation—if you don't know what you're doing, your examiner could shut your test down before you even leave the first curb. Crucial mistakes can be as simple as overcompensating while steering or mistaking the brake for the accelerator. It is better, and safer, for an examiner to end a test early than be involved in an accident with a driver who claimed to be NYS road-ready and wasn't.

Re-Dating

Other factors can stop the road test before it even starts. A road test examiner will **re-date** a road test under the following circumstances.

The examinee:
- Cannot provide proof they passed the required five-hour pre-licensing class
- Has an expired five-hour certificate
- Is 16 or 17 years old and does not have an MV262 form signed by an adult showing that they have 50 hours of supervised driving experience
- Does not have their learner's permit with them, or a photographic copy of their learner's permit, to hand to the examiner
- Has a suspended permit (which shows up when the examiner scans the permit
- Came with an accompanying driver who cannot produce a copy of their driver's license

- Is late and does not have printed confirmation of their road test booking

The vehicle being used for the test:
- Does not have a physical copy of the registration or proof of insurance to give to the examiner before the road test (though some examiners may scan the registration sticker on the windshield and let the examinee take the road test anyway)
- Has faulty tires, including those that are bald, visibly flat, and/or have broken belts
- Has improperly functioning windshield wipers and/or a cracked windshield
- Has non-functioning, or improperly functioning, seatbelts
- Has malfunctioning lights, including head and tail lights, signal lights, brake lights, etc.
- Has multiple items hanging from the rearview mirror, such as air fresheners or work badges
- Has windows so dirty that the examiner can't see from the inside of the vehicle
- The car is simply dirty
- Has shocks or springs that appear to be broken
- Is leaking fluids

- Is making noises indicating a mechanical problem (ex. screeching brakes, loud rotors/muffler, noises showing insufficient power steering fluid, etc.)
- Has a strong unpleasant smell coming from the exhaust
- Keep in mind, you can't leave the curb if your car doesn't comply with all safety laws

It is possible for an examinee holding a NYS *commercial* learner's permit to be missing some information and still take the commercial road test. In these cases, however, the examiner will not release the final results of the examinee's test until they receive the completed, requested information. Of course, once the information is received, the results are issued.

Making Mistakes

Once upon a time, road test examinees could cover for minor mistakes made during the exam by acknowledging them as they occurred. This is no longer the case. In today's road test world, apologies are no longer allowed. All examinees are expected to drive the car 100% in accordance with safety expectations, and the rules and regulations set forth by New York State.

The following is a list of common minor mistakes to watch out for while preparing for, and taking, the road test:

- Forgetting to look before taking an action
- Forgetting to signal when needed
- Palming the steering wheel
- Braking a little too hard
- Lightly touching the curb

Road tests go smoothly when examinees understand the test requirements and fulfill them automatically. Examiners are trained to pick out small weaknesses in the examinees' skills. Practicing the small things when driving (ex. visually checking blind spots, signaling and maintaining a good grip of the wheel, etc.) until they become a habit, is your best bet for road test success.

Receiving Results

A big change in recent years forbids examinees and accompanying drivers, (including the examinees' parents), from asking the examiner questions about the test once it is over. They also may not ask questions about the examinee's performance. It's up to the examiner to communicate information as they see fit. This protects the examiners' ability to perform their work in an efficient and timely manner.

In the past, road test examiners issued results to the examinee in a sealed white envelope once the test was complete. The examiner would then verbally detail the envelope's contents to the test taker. If the examinee passed successfully, the envelope would contain a white slip bearing the examiner's signature as proof of passing. If the examinee did not pass, the slip would instead list the skills the examinee needed to gain and strengthen before re-taking the road test.

Since the pandemic, however, the method examiners use to convey results to students has changed. Starting August 23, 2021, road test results were no longer given to the examinee directly after the exam. Instead, the examinee can check the results of their exam (including the list of needed skills), online after 6 PM of that same day. This new protocol serves to protect the NY State road test examiners.

During my career, I've seen multiple confrontations started by examinees who were unhappy with their road test results. The new online results reporting helps examiners avoid such confrontations. It gives them the space to do their job, and move efficiently through their test day.

Moving Forward After Road Test Failure

Many people do not pass the NYS road test the first time. If this happens to you, your best bet is to go back to your driving school (or find a driving school, if you don't have one) and re-evaluate your skills. People who fail the NYS road test twice have to pay extra fees to schedule their $3^{rd}+$ test. Forming a plan of action and working with a certified driving instructor is the best way to ensure you are properly prepared the second time around.

CHAPTER 2   THE SNOW TEST

There is an urban myth circulating that it's better to take the road test in the winter. Why? Because the examiner will give you a break due to the bad weather. This is not true. Just because it's winter, doesn't mean the examiner will go easy on you. Winter weather, however, does impact driving conditions, and the best way to stay safe is to be well prepared and to drive "gently."

Winter weather can present special challenges to road test examinees. Particularly if there's a snowstorm on the day of the scheduled exam. If visibility is horrible and the streets aren't plowed, the examinee still needs to arrive on time for their exam and successfully complete each required task.

As a professional driving instructor at the *ABC School of Driving*, I push winter driving lessons. The reason is simple—you never know when you're going to need to drive in the snow. I've known people to get stuck in the snow doing typical road test driving tasks:

- Parallel parking
- Making a 3-point turn

- Turning left or right
- Proceeding after stopping at a stop sign
- Parking on the way back to the road test's finish line
- Leaving the road test start point
- Driving straight down the road

Getting stuck happens during winter driving tests and it also happens to people after they've received their driver's license. Being a prepared driver means taking driving lessons in every type of weather—including (and especially) the worst weather. Educating yourself on how to drive for every season ensures both a successful road test and a long, SAFE driving career.

Potential Winter Road Test Problems

When preparing for a successful winter road test, it's important to learn what can go "wrong." The following are situations winter road test takers face. If you are considering a winter road test, read through these and talk to your instructor about how best to prepare.

Difficulty Executing A Safe Start To The Road Test

Winter weather often means heavily packed snow and ice on the ground. This can prevent tires from getting good traction during driving maneuvers, including starting out on your road test. Low traction can lead to spinning tires, which will get you points deducted from your exam, and could mean a NYS traffic ticket once you're licensed.

Always be aware of your situation, including the level of traction on the ground around your vehicle. Go as slow as conditions require. At all times, make sure you understand road conditions so you can maintain good vehicle control.

Gauging Safe Driving Speeds In Poor Weather

Driving speeds that would be perfectly safe and legal on a summer afternoon can become lethal in poor winter conditions. Drivers must always be aware of the interaction of their vehicle with the road and the surrounding environment. Poor weather conditions often lead to low traction, low visibility and situations requiring longer stopping times. Drivers will need to understand how to gauge safe, and often slower, driving speeds in order to keep themselves and others safe on the road in all conditions. That said, this is not only a wintertime problem. Drivers can drive too fast for conditions during the warmer months where unsafe speeds are often marked by the sound of screeching tires.

Activating The Antilock Brake System

The Antilock Brake System (ABS) is a safety back-up system designed to prevent injuries in situations where there is loss of traction and poor weather conditions, or the brakes are hit hard, and way too fast. Drivers often activate the ABS because they underestimate the interaction between the weather and the vehicle, and begin braking too late. Understanding how to gauge stopping distance and when to brake safely is vital for a successful road test. Every mistake made on the NYS road test results in points being deducted (see Chapter 3, Section 3). If a student has 30 or more points deducted, they immediately fail the test. Abrupt braking results in an automatic 10-point deduction. This leaves an examinee with only 19 points left to lose.

Sliding When Turning In Icy/Snowy Conditions

Drivers must maintain full situational awareness while approaching intersections, especially in poor weather conditions. Winter roads may be alternately wet, icy, or dry, or may be all three at once. Missing cues about the state of a road can lead to a driver taking a turn too fast for the road conditions and losing traction. This can lead to cars ending up in inappropriate places, getting stuck, or even hitting/getting hit by another car. It's the responsibility of the driver to clue into road conditions and assess the best way to execute driving tasks, no matter what the weather looks like.

Bumping Into Snowbanks While Attempting Driving Tasks

Many driving tasks require cars to maneuver near natural or man-made snow piles. These include parallel parking, 3-point turns, backing up, and basic parking, etc. In order to be safe, drivers must have good spatial awareness of where their car is in relation to the rest of the world in order to be safe. Bumping into snowbanks means: 1) The driver doesn't fully understand the dimensions (size) of their car and 2) isn't yet comfortable maneuvering the car within the space. Bumping into snowbanks can also result in a driver getting their car stuck on compacted snow.

Navigating A Traffic World Beset by Snow

Snow can make visibility very difficult during winter months, whether it's flying down from the sky or merely piled up in inconvenient places. A driver must obey all traffic signs, whether they can see them clearly or not. Even if the sky is relatively clear, snow on the ground can obstruct visibility and require drivers to go more slowly than they would in warmer months.

Man-made snow hills also make visibility very difficult at intersections. It forces drivers to pull up farther into the intersection than they normally would. In this situation, it is vital that drivers move slowly and with heightened awareness. This is the best method for dealing with an intersection with reduced visibility:

1. Come to a complete stop at the line. Observe left, right and left again behind crosswalk before moving.
2. Do not set off quickly. Instead, roll forward as slowly as possible
3. Look left and right several times, ensuring that your visibility is clear on both sides *before* you commit to the turn

4. Make your turn and go, without spinning your tires

Approaching A Yellow Light

Sometimes a driver may be approaching an intersection at an appropriately cautious speed, only to see the light turn yellow. In this situation, drivers must calculate their stopping distance and road conditions to determine whether it is safer to stop or proceed. Either way, the driver must maintain situational awareness through the entire interaction.

The best way to prepare for a winter road test—or any road test—is to take preparatory driving lessons conducted by a certified driving instructor. Certified driving instructors are trained to give student drivers customized instruction. This lets students sharpen their skills so they can safely navigate the driving world in every season. Combining rock-solid instruction with lots of practice, paves the way for a successful road test and a lifetime of safe driving.

CHAPTER 3   TEST DISQUALIFICATION

The road test should not be scary to well-prepared student drivers who are ready to drive safely. An unsuccessful exam only reflects a student's need to hone their skills before they try again. It is not a sign of future driving problems or successes. That said, there are five reasons an examinee will receive an immediate fail—a road test disqualification—during their road test.

1) Accidents

An examinee is immediately disqualified if their actions result in any situation defined by the New York State road test regulations as an "accident." The following situations result in immediate road test failure:

- Hitting the curb while attempting to turn a corner, parallel park, perform a 3-point turn, or pulling over to the curb
- Crashing into another vehicle
- Hitting a deep pothole in the road
- Hitting a person or object (no matter how small) in any gear

- Driving in such a way that the branch of a bush or tree brush up against the vehicle
- Striking an object lying in the street, such as a shoe or any type of debris
- Swerving to avoid hitting something in your travel space only to hit something else

These things are defined as accidents because they are preventable, if not "expectable." Drivers must always maintain situational awareness. This requires you to be looking as far down the road as your eyes allow you to see, while scanning for potential problems. Observational skills can and should be consistently practiced. This way, they become automatic habits and you'll be more relaxed behind the wheel.

2) Serious Traffic Violations

Committing a serious traffic violation, as defined by NYS, also results in immediate disqualification. The following list contains some of the more common traffic violations committed by road test examinees:

- Passing through a red light
- Rolling through a stop sign

- Speeding, a.k.a. driving at any speed over the sign-stated limit
- Swerving while driving
- Crooked parking, or parking so that the rear of the vehicle is in the path of other vehicles
- Cellphone use (It's a good idea to turn the phone off during the road test)
- Reckless driving
- Disobeying a traffic control device, such as a traffic signal or sign
- Having dark window tint on the windows of the car
- Neglecting to wear one's seatbelt or buckle up before departure on the road test
- Failing to signal a turn
- Making an improper turn
- Braking improperly
- Driving in the wrong direction
- Improper passing
- Changing lanes unsafely
- Failing to yield to the right of way
- Railroad crossing violations

- Using portable electronic devices other than a cell phone
- Starting unsafely, (spinning the tires in winter)

I realize that there are many items on this list that most people do not take seriously. This is a mistake. Doing any of these actions while taking your road test will result in immediate failure. Committing any of these actions *after* you receive your license gets you ticketed and violation points on either your permit or driver's license. Accumulating 11 or more violation points on a New York State driver's license results in immediate suspension of that license. Reinstating your license takes time and money. Having a suspended license in your driving history makes it more likely that future infractions will lead to a permanent loss of driving privileges.

3) Losing 30 Or More Points on The Road Test

Every mistake an examinee makes on the NYS road test results in a point deduction. Lose over 30, and you will be immediately disqualified. The following situations show that additional training is needed and can result in large point reductions:

- Not checking blind spots for potential problems
- Relying only on the mirrors to check sightlines
- Removing one's hands from the wheel while at a red light or stop sign
- Using too many maneuvers while attempting to parallel park or perform a 3-point turn
- Turning too slowly
- Driving too slowly
- Palming the steering wheel (hands should remain at the appropriate places on the wheel at all times)
- Not being able to parallel park or perform 3-point turn
- Demonstrating an inability to follow directions
- Not keeping eyes on the road
- Displaying a short-left turn or a wide right turn, often taught to students by "seasoned drivers," who have developed bad habits over time

4) Taking Dangerous Actions / Not Responding To Hazards

Drivers must always be aware of the world around them. Not being aware can lead to situations where drivers do things that endanger themselves and others. Conversely, when drivers aren't paying attention, they're likely to miss important information. This prevents them from responding appropriately to dangerous situations on and around the road. The following are examples of dangerous actions and situations that examinees need to be aware of during and after their road test.

- Swerving bicycles and/or motorcycles
- A vehicle backing out of a driveway or parking space too quickly
- Preparing the vehicle to leave the parking space without using the turn signal
- Children at play around and/or in the drivers' space of travel
- Wheel chair pedestrians riding in the street because of obstructions on the sidewalk
- Failing to pay adequate attention to visual obstructions and vehicular/pedestrian traffic at an intersection before proceeding

Anything can and will happen on the road. Being mindful of the minor details and staying alert to changing conditions keeps the driver aware of the bigger picture. After all, a driver's most important responsibility is driving safely—no matter what surprises are in store.

5) The Road Test Examiner Is Forced To Intervene During The Test

Whenever a road test examiner enters an examinee's vehicle, they are putting their safety and the safety of others into the examinee's hands. While many people are able to handle this situation, there are situations where a road test examinee fails to safely perform tasks. When this happens, it is vital for the examiner to intervene physically and/or verbally in order to maintain personal and public safety. Some examples of examiner intervention include:

- Grabbing the vehicle's steering wheel to prevent the driver from hitting something, including vehicles, pedestrians, animals, and stationary objects
- Applying the passenger-side brake (if the person taking the road test is using a driving school car)
- Verbally telling the driver to stop, wait or to not move because the examiner saw something the driver should have seen

A road test examiner's first priority is ensuring that those seeking their license are ready and prepared to drive safely at all times. For this reason, it is better to intervene and disqualify an unprepared driver than to give tacit approval to unsafe actions by passing them. That said, examiner intervention on a road test does not mean that an examinee will not successfully prepare for, and pass, a future exam. The key to future success is understanding safe driving procedures.

I once had the privilege of working with a young man who had failed his first road test. During that test, the examiner stated that the young man was about to kill someone. The young man understood at once that he was going to fail; what he didn't understand was why.

I reviewed the young man's evaluation slip from his last road test; I saw he performed most of his tasks well. That said, my colleague noted that the young man had repeatedly rolled through stop signs during the exam. Then, during his lesson with me, I learned that his father had taught him to roll through stop signs. His father had said that it was okay, as long as there was no one else in sight.

I didn't tell the young man that I too, thought he was going to kill someone with that behavior. Instead, I told him that performing that kind of "rolling stop" on the road test would mean immediate disqualification. To help him better understand, I presented him with a few scenarios and accident statistics. After all, it only takes one time for a rolling stop through a sign or light to become a vehicular manslaughter situation. By the end of our lesson, the young man both understood why the examiner had made such a dramatic statement, and he promised to never roll through a stop sign again.

The good news is that the young man passed his road test on the next try. Yes, he learned an unsafe driving practice from an "experienced" driver. Still, he did the work and corrected the problem, and now has his driver's license.

PART II

DRIVING DETAILS

CHAPTER 4 LEAVING THE CURB

While good driving practices start long before the car turns over, they kick into gear once the driver leaves the curb. Because leaving the curb and entering traffic is a key driving skill, the road test includes 3 to 4 tasks that require the examinee to leave the curb safely. Here is a list of tasks, along with the steps drivers must take to maintain safety:

1. Initial take off from curb at the start point
    a. Signal to the left. Check for pedestrians. Look left, right, shoulder checks
    b. Check each mirror in the following order: rearview; driver's side; passenger's side
    c. Check the left blind spot for oncoming traffic
    d. Turn the wheel and pull into the traffic lane

Note: Local testing practices may impact these tasks. For example, examinees taking their road test in Canandaigua, NY, start their exam in a parking lot. They then must signal to the right then perform their mirror checks, and check their right blind spot before initial take off. Do not stop on pedestrian crossings.

2. Pulling over and executing a 3-point turn
    a. While driving, signal to the right and begin to brake
    b. Shoulder check to the right
    c. Pull over to the curb
    d. Signal to the left
    e. Check the mirrors: rearview; drivers' side; passenger's side
    f. Check the left blind spot for oncoming traffic
    g. Execute the 3-point turn

3. Before and after parallel parking
    a. While driving, signal to the right and begin to brake. Shoulder check to right
    b. Pull into position
    c. Execute parallel parking
    d. When ready to reenter traffic, signal to the left
    e. Check the mirrors: rearview; driver's side and passenger side

f. Check the left blind spot for oncoming traffic

g. Turn the wheel and pull into traffic lane

4. Pulling over for an emergency vehicle and re-entering the traffic lane

   a. Determine where the emergency vehicle is approaching from—is it coming from behind or approaching from the oncoming traffic side?

   b. Signal to the right and begin to brake. Shoulder check to the right

   c. Pull over to the curb

   d. Wait for the emergency vehicle to safely pass

   e. When ready to reenter traffic, signal to the left

   f. Check the mirrors: rearview; driver's side; passenger's side

   g. Check the left blind spot for oncoming traffic and check forward traffic once more

   h. Turn the wheel and pull out into the traffic lane

Examiners love it when examinees execute a good departure from the curb, as it generally indicates that the rest of the road test is likely to go smoothly. That said, leaving the curb does have a couple of potential pitfalls. Common examinee errors at this point in the test include:

- Failing to observe (10 points deducted)
- Failing to signal (5 points deducted)
- Only using mirrors/failing to check vehicle blind spots (5 points deducted)
- Automatic fail: entering traffic when a car is coming towards you which can result in an accident

These mistakes matter because making them may cost the driver their or someone else's life. Taking care to be aware of the vehicle's environment is the best way to respond to any unexpected situations that could pop up. Keep your wits about you and watch where you're going so you and yours get there safely.

CHAPTER 5 TURNS & INTERSECTIONS

Turning seems like a simple task. You're essentially switching from driving in one direction to driving in another. Turns, however, are often made in complicated shared traffic spaces. Making a turn at the wrong time or in the wrong place can be catastrophic. Here are turning tasks every examinee should be comfortable performing BEFORE taking their road test:

- Turning into traffic from a residential driveway, whether backing or pulling out
- Exiting the traffic lane by turning left or right into a driveway, busy parking areas, or other environments outside the traffic lane
- Understanding right of way and turning at signed and lighted intersections of all types and sizes
- Entering the correct traffic lane in both one- and two-way traffic situations after making a left, or right turn at an intersection
- Moving the vehicle left or right in multi-lane highways while preparing to turn at a major intersection
- Turning while navigating school zones

- Turning left or right at intersections while following extra-large vehicles, including; tractor trailers, public transportation vehicles, school buses, construction vehicles, and dump trucks
- Turning left or right while navigating the movements of other drivers, including those who have forgotten to signal
- Understanding and navigating turning in traffic patterns, including lane shifts, roundabouts, traffic ramps, and special traffic situations
- Exiting business parking lots and turning into traffic on busy streets with multiple lanes moving in both directions
- Understanding right of way while turning left or right while navigating a railroad track
- Turning while navigating changes in traffic direction
- Turning left or right while navigating uphill or downhill traffic conditions
- Moving the car left or right in a controlled manner to avoid hitting a pothole in the middle of the street
- Changing speed while turning from, and onto, streets with variable environmental conditions,

such as a physical obstruction or children at play in and around the traffic space
- Simple lane changes
- Navigating turns while crossing bicycle-only lanes

Every one of these driving situations requires drivers to be completely aware of their surroundings. Drivers must know when to turn, how to turn, and at what speed, all while staying aware of the many vehicles, objects, and people that might get in the way of their turn. Road test examiners pay special attention to examinees' turning skills during the exam. This is especially true when approaching or waiting at an intersection.

Intersections

An intersection is defined as a point where two or more lines cross. In driving practice, it's a place where two or more traffic lanes cross where drivers need to make choices about; how, where, and how fast they're going to go. Traffic intersections and railroad crossings are usually marked by road signs and signals and are the only locations where we see stop lights. Here are some examples of common situations drivers may encounter at intersections:

- All-way stop signs
- Two-way stop signs
- Traffic signal arrays, including places with multiple lanes and turn signals
- Blinking yellow or red lights
- Railroad crossing signs indicating the presence of tracks
- Caution signs warning of hidden driveways
- Direction signs for grocery stores or shopping centers
- Signs and road markings indicating merging traffic areas
- T-intersections marked by stop or yield signs
- Stop lines on road surfaces and/or traffic signs stating "stop here"
- Entrance/exit ramps and traffic signs indicating merging traffic patterns
- Lighted and unlighted pedestrian cross-walks
- Intersecting bicycle lanes
- Roundabouts

Pay special attention to lane markings at complicated intersections! The more changes that have to happen in a limited space—whether in speed or direction—the more likely it is that problems will unexpectedly arise. Lane markings are put in place for a reason. They tell you what needs to happen, where, and when. Successful drivers need to be on the lookout for upcoming markings in order to understand all the factors at play. Only then can they figure out the best way to navigate both the markers and other drivers safely.

Getting intersections right is important, both for maintaining safety and for passing the road test. Examiners want to see road test examinees show strong observation and reaction skills at intersections. For example, a good driver can answer the following questions BEFORE their car physically arrives at the intersection:

- If at a road intersection, are there any pedestrians crossing or preparing to cross?
- Is the traffic light red, yellow, or green? If yellow, does the situation indicate I should proceed through the intersection or should I prepare to stop?
- Does the traffic light have a yellow or green arrow?

- If the light has a yellow arrow pointing left, are oncoming cars in sight that prevent me from making the turn?
- If the light is green, are there other cars, objects, vehicles, or pedestrians that may make turning difficult or unwise?
* Will present weather conditions impact my stopping time as I approach the intersection?
* Are there physical objects or blind spots that might block my view?
* At what point should I use my turn signal?
* If approaching a merging intersection, can I see cars approaching me from the side or from behind? Will I need to move my vehicle to accommodate them?

Approaching an intersection at an appropriate speed is important. It gives the driver time to observe the situation and answer these questions without causing problems for other drivers. Mirrors are often important tools for helping drivers keep their eyes on the driving situation. They are, however, no substitute for the driver turning their head and physically checking the car's blind spots. This is important at merging intersections, where it can be hard to see approaching cars until they are close to the driver's vehicle.

Navigating and Claiming the Intersection

Once the driver has arrived at an intersection, they must enter the turning space cautiously. This is especially true when making a left turn across oncoming traffic. At lighted intersections, drivers turning left need to "claim the intersection," one driver at a time.bike This means pulling forward into the center of the intersection while remaining far enough back to see the relevant traffic light. The driver may then take the turn as soon as traffic safely allows. Sometimes the light turns red while the driver is still in the intersection. This means that the driver must take their turn as soon as oncoming traffic has stopped to clear the way for other vehicles.

Staying aware

Understanding how physical environments (including the number of traffic lanes), weather, and other vehicles/pedestrians may impact each other in shared spaces is vital. The best way to learn how to navigate complex intersections is to get out and practice with a certified driving instructor. That said, the following examples show a little of the thought processes and habits good drivers need to stay safe:

Question: Can I turn right on red in a multi-lane intersection when a car coming from the opposite direction on the intersecting road has a left-turn green arrow?

Answer: Yes, carefully. A driver in the right-most lane at an intersection can safely turn right on red in this situation. After all, the car making the left turn is two lanes away. While its left-turn path takes it through the same intersection, its path does not cross the first car's path at any point. Each car in this situation must stay in their lane.

Question: What do I do if I'm driving down the right- or left-most lane on an expressway and there's a car trying to merge into my traffic lane from an entrance ramp?

Answer: It's always a good idea for a driver to turn their head and look over their shoulder as they pass entrance ramps to check for oncoming traffic. Unfortunately, there are people in this world who are not knowledgeable about safely entering expressways.

Getting eyes on an approaching car gives you the chance to respond to a potentially negative situation BEFORE they're in your driving space. It also allows you the chance to adjust your vehicle's speed and/or road position to allow the other car to merge safely. Remember, mirrors are useful, but they are NOT a substitute for turning your head and looking.

Common intersection errors on the road test

Here is a list of common errors student drivers make, as well as points deducted, navigating intersections during the New York State Road Test:

- Stopping at intersections when there is a stop sign or light
- Showing poor judgment while approaching or at the intersection (10 points)
- Forgetting to signal before making a turn (5 points)
- Signaling at the wrong time (5 points)
- Approaching/moving through the intersection too fast or too slow (10 points)
- Making turns that are too short or too wide for the situation (5 to 10 points)

- Making right or left turns so wide the car ends up in the left lane of the intersecting road, risking head-on collision (30 points/Immediate failure)
- Traveling over a speed hump faster than coasting speed/5 mph (5 or more points)
- Stopping at a green light (30 points/Immediate failure)
- Failing to stop at a red light (30 points/Immediate failure)
- Failing to observe and respond to driving conditions (10 points)
- Failing to claim the intersection appropriately (10 or more points)
- Failing to stop near center of intersection while making a left turn
- Not paying attention to traffic signs, signals, and lane markings (5 points per instance)
- Crossing lane markings
    - Single solid white line (10 points per tire)
    - Double yellow line (20 points per tire)
    - Stop line near a stop sign or signal
    - Bicycle lane markings
    - School crossing lane markings
    - Turning lane markings

As always, it is vital for drivers to remain alert and aware of their driving situation at all times. While driving straight, drivers should see and read every single traffic sign in their travel path. They must also respond appropriately. Failing to do so can cost student drivers their road test, and lead experienced drivers to have dangerous—and fully preventable—accidents.

To pass the NYS road test, an examinee needs to lose fewer than 29 points. Make sure you are prepared for every task the examiner will ask you to do. It is totally possible for an examinee to perform perfectly on the open road, only to lose 85+ points by cutting an intersection short and hitting the center yellow line with all four tires. My goal, both as road test examiner and certified driving instructor, is to help drivers think about what's they need to know and do *before* they get to that road test.

CHAPTER 6

PARKING, BACKING & U-TURNS

It's easy to think that driving is just about going from one place to another in a car. Besides staying in their lane, drivers also need to know how to correct course, and their maneuver vehicles in and out of a variety of parking situations. These situations require the driver to understand where their car is in space, as well as how to accelerate and brake safely in potentially small spaces. All drivers are required to parallel park and perform a broken-U, or three-point turn, in order to pass the NYS road test.

Parking

Parking is the act of maneuvering one's vehicle into a designated parking space. Drivers need to navigate different parking situations comfortably, including street-side parking; designated straight, angled, and unmarked parking spaces in lots and/or garages; and residential/commercial driveways. Safe parking often requires maneuvering a big vehicle in and out of small spaces without damaging nearby people and property. This requires the driver to juggle several essential tasks while moving the vehicle. The driver must:

- Identify an available parking space
- Use turn signals to let nearby drivers and pedestrians know that you will be maneuvering into the parking space
- Check for oncoming/conflicting traffic using vehicle mirrors and turning your head for visual confirmation
- Show appropriate vehicle control to enter the parking space without hitting nearby vehicles, pedestrians, objects, and/or parking barriers
- Maintain appropriate distance from other vehicles/pedestrians
- Avoid hitting other cars, pedestrians, curbs, and objects when opening doors after the car has come to a complete stop and the engine has been shut off

Parallel parking

Simple parking can be challenging for many drivers. Parallel parking requires another level of driver ability and awareness. Most motor vehicles are designed to move back and forth along a linear path. Parallel parking requires the driver to take those vehicles and shift them sideways. To parallel park, a driver must:

- Identify an available parking space and signal to show that they will maneuver into the parking space
- Check for oncoming/conflicting traffic using vehicle mirrors and turning your head for visual confirmation
- Pull forward alongside the space in front of the parking space and stop parallel to the curb. If there is another vehicle present, it is often a good idea to line up the vehicles' side mirrors or rear ends. This helps the driver line up in preparation for parallel parking maneuvers
- Shift the vehicle into reverse and use appropriate acceleration, turning, and braking techniques to angle the car first towards, and then back into the space.
- Ease the vehicle into the space (maintaining the legally appropriate distance from the curb) without hitting other vehicles, objects, the curb, or pedestrians
- Straighten the wheels and pull slightly forward, straightening the vehicle so that it is physically parallel to the curb at all points
- Shift into park

- Visually check the surrounding area to check for passersby to avoid hitting into them when opening doors after the car has come to a complete stop/been shut off

Parallel parking is one of the more difficult maneuvers drivers are required to master. Because of this, student drivers learning to parallel park will strongly benefit from certified professional instruction. The skills required to parallel park are the same skills that make the difference between passing and failing the NYS road test. Perfecting those skills with a certified instructor will pay dividends both at the road test and throughout the driver's life.

Common parallel parking mistakes

Parking a vehicle is an essential skill. As a result, road test examiners pay special attention to a would-be driver's parking skills. Remember, a hopeful driver needs 30 out of 40 points to pass the drivers' licensing exam. It only takes a few minor mistakes to take a driver from passing to failing. Here is a list of common mistakes student drivers make during their NYS road test and their deduction point values:

- Failure to signal (5 points)
- Failure to adequately observe caution (10 points)
- Parking too far from curb (5 points)
- Failure to park properly (15 points)
    - Failing to straighten vehicle after reversing direction
    - Failing to shift into park after parallel parking and indicating to the examiner that the parallel park was complete
    - Completing the park too far from the curb
    - Displaying too many maneuvers (forward and backing movements) while trying to park
    - Moving too close to neighboring vehicles while parking or preparing to parallel park
    - Remaining too far into the traffic lane while preparing to park, preventing approaching vehicles from safely passing
    - Forgetting the required steps for parallel parking
    - Failing to maintain signaling throughout parking maneuvers (Note: Signals sometimes turn themselves off, requiring the driver to turn them back on)

- Accelerating too quickly while attempting to park
- Hitting the curb while attempting to parallel park
- Moving too far forward to line up the vehicles' mirrors and/or rear end while preparing to parallel park
- Failing to look in the right direction while the vehicle was moving
- Turning the steering wheel in the wrong direction before parallel parking, forcing the examiner to grab the steering wheel and end the road test
- Palming the steering wheel
- Moving the vehicle in the path of other oncoming vehicles

Broken U-turns/Three-point turns/K-turns

There are many times throughout a driver's life when they will need to stop going one way and start going another. It is often possible to turn around in a nearby driveway and/or parking lot (also referred to as a two-point turn). When it isn't, drivers also need to know how to turn around on the road itself. The best way to accomplish this is to perform a broken-U turn.

"What exactly is a broken-U turn?" you might ask. This is a question Road Examiners get often, as the broken-U turn has several names—broken-U turn, three-point turn, and K-turn. Each name, in its own way, refers to the steps a driver needs to take to do the turn. Would-be drivers should know all three names to be prepared for the road test. I've had a number of students who have learned the names and steps for the broken-U in my 5-hour prep class, only to have their brains go blank at the road test. Remember, a road test examiner may use ANY of these names during the exam. Using the different names and practicing maneuvers with a certified driving instructor will ensure you show up ready to go.

The maneuver

Performing a broken-U turn requires the driver to:

- Check the area for oncoming/conflicting traffic using vehicle mirrors
- Turn your head for direct visual confirmation

- Signal right, indicating to other drivers and pedestrians that the driver is moving right to prepare for the turn
- Pull towards the right-hand curb, coming to a stop
- Re-check the area for oncoming/conflicting traffic using vehicle mirrors
- Turn your head for visual confirmation
- Signal left to indicate the car will be moving left
- Turn the steering wheel towards the left and pulling the car across the traffic lanes, angling towards the opposite direction before coming to a stop
- Turn the steering wheel towards the right, and turn your head for visual confirmation of a clear path before shifting into reverse
- Back/straighten the vehicle into the traffic lane
- Pull forward and continue driving in the new direction

Common broken-U turn mistakes

Failing to implement the broken-U turn correctly is an automatic 15-point deduction on the NYS road test. The road test may continue after that point, but the examinee will not be getting their license. To avoid this failure, it's vital to avoid these common mistakes examinees make during the broken-U, or three-point, turn:

- Not knowing how to perform a broken-U turn
- Failing to signal right at the beginning of the turn to alert vehicles approaching from the front or back
- Turning into the left traffic lane without signaling to the left, checking mirrors, or checking the left blind spot over the left shoulder
- Pulling into a driveway and performing a two-point turn instead of performing the broken-U turn
- Not looking where you should be, before and while the vehicle is in motion
- Using too many maneuvers to complete the three-point turn
- Hitting the curb at any point during the turn, including while pulling forward or reversing the vehicle
- Not being able to identify the three names associated with a 3-point turn:
  1. 3-Point Turn
  2. K-Turn
  3. Broken U-turn

4. Blocking of Impeding Traffic for a Long Time

CHAPTER 7   VEHICLE CONTROL

According to the United States' census bureau (June 2023), there are 286 million vehicles operating on American roads. There are roughly 20 million traffic stops each year. In 2022, the National Highway Traffic Safety Association (NHSTA) reported 42,795 fatalities due motor vehicle crashes. Drivers must have good control over their vehicles in all driving situations—it is literally a matter of life and death.

Still, what does it mean to have good vehicle control? Vehicle control is the sum of all of driving's parts. It includes the ability to maneuver the vehicle without hitting other things while obeying traffic laws and regulations. It also includes having good control over the vehicle's mechanical processes at all times. Basic tasks (ex. staying in your lane, starting/stopping, and proper shifting require, etc.) require as high a level of control as complicated ones. No text can cover every point of vehicle control. That said, this chapter focuses on some of the more common challenges student drivers face when preparing for, and taking, the NYS road test.

Developing steering control

The best way to describe good steering control is to say that it's *comfortable.* When a driver has good steering control, every maneuver they attempt in their vehicle is made at the right time, at the right speed. Neither the driver nor the passengers feel like they're being tossed about the car. Instead, everyone feels physically comfortable at every point during the driving experience.

Driving straight

A driver's first priority when practicing good steering control is learning how to stay comfortably in their lane. This begins with learning how to drive straight. Driving straight requires you to stay comfortably in the center of your traffic lane without drifting too far or too close to either side. It seems simple enough—until you deal with challenges like rough roads and misaligned vehicles. Of course, driving straight is one of the first and most important skills a student learns from their certified driving instructor. Keeping a vehicle in its proper lane:

- Prevents motor vehicle accidents by ensuring every person in the driving situation knows where the vehicle is

- Sets up the vehicle to turn properly as needed
- Makes it possible for the driver to maneuver around unexpected objects/people/problems in the traffic lane

During the NYS road test, failing to drive straight is referred to as "improper lane of traffic." This means that the person taking the road test was unable to keep the vehicle driving on a straight path. This can cost the examinee 10 points. Given that an examinee only has 30 points to lose before they fail, it may seem like you could still pass after getting points deducted for improper lane of traffic. Unfortunately, a person who cannot perform this essential vehicle control skill is likely to fail at other tasks. I haven't known many people who have this problem on their test and still managed to pass.

Turning

It's important to maintain steering control during left and right turns. During the turn, drivers should maneuver their vehicles with a comfortable motion, keeping the car at a speed that is neither too fast nor too slow. The driver and the passengers in the car should feel just as physically comfortable throughout the turn as they do when the driver is driving straight. Taking turns too quickly exerts uncomfortable physical forces on both the passengers and the vehicle. Drivers who struggle to steer comfortably may repeatedly overcorrect their steering. This makes the vehicle jerk in unexpected directions, jamming passengers around the cabin. It also creates an unpredictable and dangerous situation for nearby drivers and pedestrians.

It shouldn't surprise you that drivers with poor steering control are more likely to lose control and cause an accident/collision. Road test examiners are committed to maintaining public safety. As a result, they pay special attention to an examinee's steering control skills during the NYS road test. If the examiner is not comfortable with the way the examinee is steering the vehicle, they will deduct 15 points or immediately end the exam. Either way, it means that the examinee has failed.

Failure to keep right

In most countries around the world, traffic moves forward on the right-hand side of the highway. Keeping right means staying with the flow of traffic on the right side of the highway. "Failure to keep right," therefore, happens when a driver makes a turn at an intersection and does NOT remain in (or even enter) the proper lane once the turn is completed.

A minor instance of failure to keep right results in a 10-point deduction on the road test. Anything above "minor" can result in immediate failure. Why? Because turning left or right and ending up on the left-hand side of the highway can cause a head-on motor vehicle collision. It also counts as a dangerous action, as noted earlier in this book. These are two of the five situations listed on the NYS road test as reasons for immediate disqualification. This is why drivers who fail to stay in their correct lane while turning are highly likely to fail their road test.

As always, the best way to ensure a good result on the road test and in life is to book one or more driving lessons with a certified driving instructor. An experienced instructor will quickly zero in on the places you need to strengthen your steering control skills. Their insight will make your practice more efficient and effective.

Changing lanes

Lane changes can come up fast. Changing road conditions and navigation needs often require drivers to change lanes at the drop of a hat. The physical act of moving from lane to lane seems simple enough.

Changing lanes, however, can be very dangerous if you are not fully aware of the variables in your driving environment. This is especially true in high-speed and/or heavy traffic conditions.

There are four things a driver MUST do to be safe while changing lanes:

1) Signal towards the lane the driver is changing to (right if moving right, and left if moving left)
2) Check the rearview mirror to see if there are vehicles approaching from behind in the destination lane
3) Check the side-view mirror to see if there are vehicles blocking the path into the destination lane
4) Turn head around and check the vehicle's blind spot to see if other vehicles blocking the path into the destination lane

Forgetting any of these steps means automatic point deductions on the NYS road test. Forgetting them all means failure.

When practicing lane changes, keep in mind that the above steps must be followed every time a driver moves from one lane to the next. A driver in the far-right lane of an expressway with 3+ lanes going in one direction must not simply signal once and swoop to the other side. That can cause a serious accident. To stay safe, drivers must change lanes one at a time, repeating every necessary step each time they move over a lane. This gives the driver precious time to monitor and respond to unexpected change in the driving environment. It also gives other drivers the time they need to do the same.

Pulling over

There are many times when the situation forces a driver to stop their vehicle while still on the road. The safest way to do this is to pull the vehicle over. Pulling over for passing emergency vehicles gives them space to do their jobs. A driver can, and should, pull over when they need a safe moment to turn their attention away from the road. Pulling over to the shoulder gives law enforcement officers a temporary place to enforce traffic law. Finally, pulling over can be a useful tool for improving your driving situation by giving other vehicles space. When pulling over, a driver must:

1) Signal to the right (or left, in the advent of an emergency on a multi-lane highway)

2) Check both the rearview mirror and passenger side view mirror for potential obstacles
3) Look over their right (or left) shoulder to visually check the vehicle's blind spot
4) Pull the vehicle over to the right (or left)
5) Bring the vehicle to a full stop and shifting the vehicle into "park"

Right of way

"Right of way" is the set of rules drivers use to know who gets to move and when. It provides guidelines that help drivers navigate the road without endangering themselves or others. For the most part, right of way is indicated by the traffic markings, signs, and signals in the driving environment. For example, when two vehicles stop at the same time at a signed 4-way intersection, the rule is to let the vehicle on the right take the intersection first. This helps prevent drivers from getting confused and/or getting into an accident.

Right of way also applies when drivers have to share space with pedestrians and cyclists. In many situations, pedestrians have the right of way. This means the driver must slow or stop their vehicle so the pedestrian can use the road space to continue their journey. Remember, motor vehicles serve as a sort of armor, protecting the driver and passengers from outside objects. Pedestrians (and cyclists) don't have that protection. Failing to yield to the pedestrians' right of way by cutting them off or failing to notice them entering the space is a 15-point deduction on the road test.

Staying aware of other people and animals in the driving environment is vitally important for respecting right of way and keeping people safe. Any person, object, or living creature can blast into view, interfering with drivers' ability to make timely driving decisions. Drivers must be careful and look as far as they can down the street. This is how you give yourself the opportunity to see what is happening around you and respond before you get to the point of no return.

Maintaining appropriate speed

Traffic works best when it flows. This means that all the vehicles on the road are moving smoothly, going neither too fast nor too slow for the conditions. Gauging appropriate speed is a vital driving skill. Moving a vehicle too slowly can cause problems during maneuvers or block the appropriate flow of traffic. Moving too quickly, however, increases drivers' chances of accidents and collisions. In addition, accidents and collisions at higher speeds are more likely to result in severe injury and even death. Maintaining appropriate speed isn't just good for passing the road test—it's good for staying alive.

Driving too slow

Driving too slowly impedes traffic flow and can confuse or frustrate, other drivers. Many of us have seen that one car crawling along on the highway with a long line of vehicles crunched up behind them, the driver puttering along as if lost in a dream. If the roads and skies are clear and the driving conditions are good, driving 10-15 miles under the speed limit is too slow. Often, other drivers will respond by honking their horn and passing—sometimes without regard for mutual safety. Driving too slowly can also mean that faster-moving vehicles are more likely to enter the shared space too quickly for anyone to react. Examiners will note these situations when they occur during the road test and deduct points accordingly.

Many long-term drivers insist that the safest way to drive is with the flow of traffic. I agree—but only to a point. It is best to drive with the flow of traffic *as long as the driver respects the posted speed limit.* Believe it or not, people will still pass you when you're going the limit!

Examiners, however, value safe driving and will not the unsafe actions of others against the examinee.

Poor engine control

Sometimes examinees will have points deducted on their road test for "poor engine control" or "poor acceleration." This simply means that they cannot keep their vehicle traveling at the exact speed limit. For example, if the posted speed limit says 30 mph, you should be driving consistently at about 30 mph. It is very impressive when a driver maintains the exact speed limit for their entire exam. That said, most examiners will accept speeds from 2 to 3 mph below the limit, though they prefer the driver to either be at the exact limit to 1 mph above.

Understanding "excessive speed"

Legal speed limits mark the maximum speed a driver can go while maintaining a safe road environment for themselves and others. Even then, sometimes going the speed limit is actually going too fast. Weather, traffic, and road conditions all impact safe driving speeds, and the more challenging the conditions are, the slower a driver needs to go. On the NYS road test, examiners dock

10 points every time an examinee uses speeds "excessive for weather, traffic, or road conditions."

The NYS road test requires examinees to lose no more than 29 points. Many examinees do the math and figure that they can still pass after losing 10 points. (Translation, they can speed once and still get their license.) That might be true, numbers wise, but the number of points you lose depends on what took place when you lost them. You *might* be fine if you did the maneuver a little too fast. If the examiner deducted points because you pushed your vehicle above the posted speed limit, however, you should technically fail. Why? Because according to the law, exceeding the speed limit by even 1 mph is speeding and a traffic violation. NYS law states that it's the driver's responsibility to maintain the posted limit. Even fully licensed drivers can be ticketed and receive violation points for going 1 or more miles per hour above the limit.

Tips for maintaining speed during the road test
- Drive according to the posted speed limit
- Keep a steady pace in good or bad weather
- Don't cancel the test if the weather is bad

- Travel slower in negative conditions and don't compromise safety to make other drivers happy

I cannot overstress how important it is for examinees to get quality practice time with their certified driving instructor before taking their test. At ABC School of Driving, we always pick up our examinees 45 minutes prior to their road test. This allows them to cram a little practice in and rectify things that could cost them the entire test. There are times, however, when 45 minutes just isn't enough. Commit your time and resources to getting good-quality driving instruction and practice. It is the best way to make road test day a success.

Braking safely

When driving or riding along on a nice day, it is easy to forget that motor vehicles are large, heavy objects subject to the laws of physics. The size, shape, speed, and weight of a vehicle affects the way the vehicle handles—including how fast it comes to a stop. Common sense dictates that heavy vehicles take longer to stop than lighter ones. The driver of a large SUV, therefore, probably needs to start braking farther away from the final stop point than the driver of a compact sedan.

Slippery weather conditions can also impact stop time, as can the state of the vehicle's tires or the condition of the pavement.

Failing to brake well can easily result in an accident, making safe braking a vital vehicle control skill. NYS road test examiners check examinees' skills by paying attention to whether or not their braking is delayed and/or abrupt. Yet what does delayed/abrupt braking mean?

When braking is delayed or abrupt, it means that you have taken too long to apply their brakes when stopping. As a result, the brakes are applied too hard and too fast, making the vehicle jerk one or more times while stopping. In imperfect driving conditions, delayed/abrupt braking can mean that your vehicle does not stop by the stopping point. The last thing you want is to slide past the sign/signal/stop point into the path of oncoming traffic because you hit the brakes too late. Delayed/abrupt braking can also cause your vehicle car to lose traction in slippery road conditions. This makes it more likely that you will lose control of their vehicle and get into an accident.

The best way to brake safely starts with slightly touching the brake pedal as soon as you know you will be stopping. You can then keep your foot on the pedal and apply gradual pressure to the brake, easing the car to a safe and comfortable stop. As always, the best way to perfect your braking skills is to get real-world experience during a lesson with a certified driving instructor.

Shifting smoothly

All road-safe motor vehicles in the United States have a transmission that allows them to gain and reduce speed efficiently while driving. Vehicles with automatic transmissions have a built-in system that shifts gears for the driver in almost every situation. Vehicles with manual transmissions, however, are a little more complicated. They require the driver to coordinate the clutch, brake, and gas pedals with the stick shift while driving.

Using the clutch

Drivers of manual transmission vehicles must always start the car in first gear. First gear transmits the most force from the engine to the wheels, thus providing the power the vehicle needs to begin moving. As the vehicle increases in speed, the driver must "shift up," moving from gear to higher gear. Doing this allows the transmission to moderate transfer of energy from the engine to the wheels. Lower gears provide slow-moving power, while higher gears are best for efficiently turning fuel into speed.

When shifting gears, it may help to remember that the gear number should match the first digit of the vehicle's speed in miles per hour (mph). For example, drivers start their vehicles in first gear, which covers speeds from 1 to 19 mph. When the vehicle hits 20 mph, the driver should use the clutch to shift into 2nd gear. Third gear comes at 30 mph, and 4th gear at 40 mph.

Poor use of gears

It is possible to shift poorly in automatic and manual transmission vehicles. In an automatic vehicle, "poor use of gears" often means that the driver attempted to start and/or accelerate the vehicle without first putting it "Drive." It can also mean that the driver forgot to shift into "Reverse," or shifted into "Reverse" at the wrong time. This is very easy to do during multiple-maneuver tasks like parallel parking and the broken U-turn. Occasionally, an examiner will give an examinee a break on this if the test-taker immediately catches their mistake and acknowledges it. If the examinee hits the curb because they forgot to shift, or shifted inappropriately, however, NYS regulations require the examiner to call it a motor vehicle accident and fail the driver immediately.

Poor use of gears as described above can also be a problem in manual vehicles. In addition, manual drivers can display poor clutch control. This is the inability to synchronize working the clutch, gas, and brake pedals in order to shift smoothly. Poor clutch control in a manual vehicle often shows up during the road test with the sound of scraping gears.

Repeated stalling

Repeated stalling in a motor vehicle can cost you 10 points on the road test. What, however, does "repeated stalling" even mean? A car stalls when the engine stops working the way it should. This can happen in all vehicles. In manual transmission vehicles, it can happen when you cannot put the car properly in gear when starting the vehicle. Repeated stalling is a prime example of poor vehicle control and will result in losing points on the road test.

Analyzing and responding to road conditions

Good judgment is a driver's number one most important skill. Having good judgment is essential for passing the road test, as it only takes three small lapses in judgment (10 points apiece) to fail the exam. It is even more essential to drive safely throughout your life. When I'm teaching driving, I always like to use stopping distance as my example of how to make a good judgment call on the road. Why? Because most people who cause a rear end collision hit the car in front of them because they were too close to stop on time. Under NYS regulations, following the vehicle in front of you too closely (a.k.a. tailgating) gets you a traffic ticket and 4 driver violation points against your license. New York drivers who receive 11 or more points during an 18-month period will have their license suspended.

Exercising good driving judgment starts with the paying attention to all the variables in one's environment: weather; road conditions; vehicle and foot traffic; construction; traffic signs, signals, and markers; lighting/visibility; moving objects and debris; dangerous actors; road closures; large public events; etc. Every change in the environment affects driving safety. Good drivers constantly scan the road and its surroundings for potential problems. Catching a problem early gives drivers time to figure out how, and when, they need to respond. Even a few milliseconds of warning can mean the difference between life and death in a challenging driving environment.

Reacting to emergencies

Catastrophic things happen on the road every day. Sometimes they happen in the blink of an eye. For example, you may be driving straight down the road when a vehicle in front of you suddenly backs out of a driveway into your lane. What do you do? Perhaps you don't do anything. Perhaps you continue to drive straight because you have right away, and you don't even honk your horn at the vehicle backing out of the driveway.

What happens then?

On the NYS road test, examiners deduct points for "poor reaction to emergencies." This means that the examinee did not appropriately respond to a potentially dangerous driving situation. In the above example, driving straight without honking the horn is an example of a poor reaction. Why? Because it could easily end with you slamming into the other vehicle at high speed. Both vehicles could be destroyed and both drivers seriously injured—maybe even killed.

Here's another example. You're at the beginning of your road test, and you're tempted to move your vehicle. You check your mirrors, and because you don't see anything, you start driving. Suddenly, the examiner grabs the wheel, stopping you as a car wooshes by, barely missing you. You realize that car had been in your blind spot. If you'd only turned your head, you'd have seen it.

In this example, you don't react to the emergency because you don't see it in the first place. On the NYS road test, this also counts as another example of poor reaction to emergency. Why? Because if the examiner had not intervened, your lack of observation and reaction would have caused one.

Poor reaction to emergency matters. According to the National Safety Council's website in 2023, preventable injuries are the 4th leading cause of death in the United States. A high number of those injuries happen in motor vehicle accidents. According to Forbes.com, there were over 5.2 million motor vehicle accidents in the U.S. during 2020, and 35,766 of them were fatal. Failing to look means failing to observe. Failing to observe means failing to react, so people and property get damaged—sometimes past the point of repair.

The best way for drivers to avoid poor reaction to emergency on their road test is to practice observation and awareness at all times. Scan the environment at all times while turning your head to look as far down the road as the eye will allow you to see. Enlist the help of a certified driving instructor to identify and fix bad driving habits. Above all, be mindful how small actions, or the lack thereof, could potentially cause an accident or a fatality. Stay mindful of all these things, and you will continue to drive alive.

A note on readiness (a.k.a. checking in before the test)

New drivers are often very excited about getting their license and often want to rush to take the road test. While this is understandable, it's best to think of a safe driving career as a marathon—not a sprint. While it might feel good to blast off the starting block, good driving skills have to be built over time through dedicated practice. It's best for student drivers to clock as many hours as possible practicing their skills with a certified driving instructor. This gives new drivers the time and guidance they need to establish the driving habits they need to keep themselves (and others) safe.

Checking in with the instructor can also save a potential examinee a lot of embarrassment. As a road test examiner and driving instructor, I have often had to be the person who tells the examinee they aren't prepared to pass. No one wants to hear that their road test should be converted to a driving lesson. It's is particularly for so-called "seasoned drivers," otherwise known as examinees who were *so sure* they were ready to get their license. If I could piece of advice to road test hopefuls, it would be this. Even if you have a good feeling that you could pass that road test today, check in with your driving instructor. They'll know if you're ready to pass or if you need a little more work. Either way, they'll do what it takes to help you succeed.

Common road test errors

To sum up, here is a list of common vehicle control errors examinees make on the NYS road test:

- Repeated stalling (10-point deduction)
- Poor engine control/acceleration (10-point deduction)
- Poor steering control while driving straight, turning, and executing maneuvers (15-point deduction)
- Delayed/abrupt breaking (10-point deduction)
- Poor use of gears in automatic or manual transmission vehicles (10-point deduction)
- Poor clutch control (5-point deduction)

- Poor reaction to emergencies 10-point deduction
- Fails to keep right (10-point deduction)
- Improper lane of traffic (10-point deduction)
- Follows too closely (10-point deduction)
- Speed excessive for traffic, weather, and road conditions (15-point deduction)
- Driving too slow/impeding traffic flow (15-point deduction)
- Fails to yield to the right of way of pedestrians/other (15-point deduction)
- Fails to anticipate the action of pedestrians or other (10-point deduction)
- Poor judgment in traffic (10-point deduction)
- Fails to signal, observe or use caution when changing lanes (10-point deduction)
- Fails to signal (5-point deduction)
- Fails to use caution (10-to-30-point deduction, depending on the situation)
- Poor judgment in traffic
    - Fails to maintain appropriate speed
    - Fails to observe (10-point deduction)
    - Fails to stop at appropriate speed/distance

- Fails to anticipate the actions of pedestrians or others

CHAPTER 8   WHEN STOP MEANS STOP

Every day, millions of people use New York State roads to get where they need to go. On their way, those people will encounter a variety of traffic situations and people. They will have to deal with pedestrians, cyclists, playing children, and law enforcement/emergency personnel. All of those people have friends and families of their own. All of those people deserve to go home safe. Traffic control regulations, devices, and enforcement officers work together to make that happen.

When STOP means stop

Red lights and stop signs are the most recognizable traffic control devices used today. Even children know the red sign with the white letters means "STOP RIGHT NOW." Red lights and signs, however, are only two of the traffic devices that tell us to stop. There are also sirens and flashing lights. These show up on crossings, construction zones, transport vehicles, and emergency vehicles. They tell us something important is happening and that we need to help by stopping and getting out of the way.

To be clear, when we are talking about stopping a vehicle, we are talking about applying the vehicle's brakes until it is no longer moving in any direction. Slowing down to a crawl and rolling through a stop does not count as stopping. Neither does bringing the vehicle to a brief pause, only to go again. Stopping definitely does not mean continuing to drive in the vague hope that the flashing lights behind or in front of you will magically disappear.

"STOP" always means stop—full stop. Stop means stop when:

- Driving your car and you're approaching a stop sign or red light
- Encountering a red light while navigating a cross walk
- Approaching an all-way stop when you know that you don't have right of way unless you arrive at the stop sign first
- Approaching a 2-way stop sign when the people traveling from the left or right side have no stop sign

- Emergency/law enforcement vehicles approach from the front or back while you are driving in the traffic lane

    When this happens, always signal to the right and pull over to the shoulder before stopping.

- You're driving down the street and see a yield sign while traffic is approaching from the left or right
- You approach an intersection to make a left turn against oncoming traffic without a green right-of-way arrow (see the section about claiming the intersection)
- Approaching an intersection to make a right turn where the light is red

    After stopping and checking that no traffic is coming from the left, drivers can make a careful right turn at a red light unless there is a sign stating "No turn on red."

- Approaching a railroad crossing with red flashing lights and/or arms coming down to block traffic

    In this situation, you may hear a loud horn. This means a train is coming. Failing to obey stop signals at a railroad crossing means your vehicle will end up in the train's path.

- Driving down the street while looking as far as the eye can see, and observing an animal or small child dart into the street (make sure the situation behind you is safe)
- Driving and observing nearby pedestrians and cyclists swerving in and out of traffic, endangering you and other around you
- A family of ducks or geese cross the road in front of your vehicle
- Flashing lights on large-scale vehicles such as garbage trucks and school buses indicate the need to stop

Dealing with extra-large vehicles

We've already discussed how physics means large vehicles take longer to stop than smaller vehicles. Large vehicles also require more space to maneuver and much longer sightlines. It makes sense, therefore, that extra-large vehicles—including tractor trailers, construction/utility/farm vehicles, school/public transportation busses, trams, trolleys, garbage trucks, and tow trucks—would need even more than your average pickup or SUV.

As a general rule, if you can't see the side view mirrors on the vehicle in front of you, that vehicle's driver can't see you. This is especially true for extra-large vehicles. This becomes a particular problem when extra-large vehicles need to stop quickly or maneuver in tight driving conditions. Any vehicles following too closely behind them risk a dangerous, costly, and potentially fatal rear end collision. You also risk getting pulled over by law enforcement and receiving a hefty fine and 4 violation points on their driver's license. The best way for you to stay safe (and traffic-ticket free) is to give the vehicles in front of you plenty of space—especially when those vehicles are extra-large. If giving space is hard for any reason, your best bet is to pull over to a stop and give the other driver a chance to pull away.

Sometimes you need to stop

In this section, we've covered a lot of situations where something outside the car, like a signal or a person, forces the driver to stop. There are also times when a driver needs to stop because of things happening *inside* the vehicle. Passengers and cell phones can be distracting. Thoughts and feelings and physical fatigue can distract, too. This is a problem. Why? Because a distracted driver is less likely to see what's going on around them and respond on time. They are also more likely to make poor driving choices because their ability to think clearly is impaired.

Most people understand they need to show up for their road test well-rested. Being tired behind the wheel, however, is a problem that can (and will) crop up throughout a driver's career. It is also a much bigger deal than most people realize. Studies indicate that being too tired can cause the same brain- and body-impairments as drinking alcohol. According to the CDC[1], being awake for 17 hours (ex. from 6:00 am to 11:00 pm) has the same impact on brain and body functioning as having a Blood Alcohol Content of 0.05%. Twenty-four hours awake brings that number up to 0.10%—.02% higher than the legal cut-off for dangerous intoxication in the United States. The National Highway Traffic Safety Administration (NHTSA) found[2] that fatigue (a.k.a. drowsy driving) caused more than 91,000 police-reported accidents in 2017. That same year, a study from Australia[3] found that young people ages 18-24 were

---

[1] https://www.cdc.gov/niosh/work-hour-training-for-nurses/longhours/mod3/08.html, July 2023
[2] https://www.nhtsa.gov/risky-driving/drowsy-driving, July 2023
[3] https://pubmed.ncbi.nlm.nih.gov/28859144/, July 2023

overrepresented in drowsy-driving statistics. This means younger drivers are more likely than older drivers to hurt themselves and others by driving tired.

Highway hypnosis is another fatigue-related problem that can show up when a driver has been on the road too long. Many roads (especially multi-lane highways) can look the same mile after mile. The monotony of seeing and doing the things over and over can lull a driver's brain into a relaxed, half-aware state. Studies suggest that this can happen within 20 minutes after a driver begins their journey. The chances of experiencing highway hypnosis go up when drivers are already tired[4]. Feeling relaxed and half-aware is fine when you're kicking back at home. On the road, it is a recipe for motor vehicle disaster.

To sum up, safe drivers are self-aware drivers. They know when it's time to throw in the towel and stop driving. Here are a few examples of driver situations where stop has to mean STOP:

---

[4] https://www.healthline.com/health/highway-hypnosis, July 2023

- Been on the road too long (as a general rule, drivers on long trips should take a minimum 15-minute break after every 2 hours of driving)
- Being too stressed, angry, confused, panicked, and/or tired, to drive calmly
- Being too physically ill or injured to pay attention to the road environment, and/or operate the pedals and steering wheel safely
- Being too distracted by passengers, technology, thoughts, feelings, or events to be fully calm and aware of the road while driving

If (and when) any of these things ever become an issue during your driving career, do yourself a favor and pull your vehicle over and park. Grab a bus, or call an Uber, a taxi, or a friend to pick you up. It is easier, cheaper, and more convenient to pick your car up the next day than to recover from a preventable accident.

CHAPTER 9

LAW ENFORCEMENT ON THE ROAD

Every day, thousands of people are pulled over by law enforcement while driving. While many people associate being pulled over with speeding, there are many reasons may legally pull a driver over. Here are the top 10 reasons for traffic stops:

1) Speeding

   This is the most common reason for traffic stops. The NHTSA reports that speeding drivers in the U.S. caused 9717 fatalities in 2017—or a quarter of all traffic fatalities for that year.

2) Vehicle defects

   This can include bad/broken lights and other visible vehicle defects. According to the NHTSA, 2% of all vehicle crashes are due to mechanical defects. These include issues like bad brakes, steering defects, acceleration issues, bad signal lights, bad headlights, bad tail lights, bad brake lights, and weak batteries.

3) Record checks

One in 10 traffic stops is due to record checks. At these times, the police officer will use the computer in their vehicle to look up the driver's license record on the law enforcement database. These stops are less likely to result in a ticket vehicle search or arrest than others.

4) Illegal turns

   Making an illegal turn or lane change of any kind counts as a traffic violation. According to the NHTSA, this kind of violation accounts for 6.8% of all traffic stops.

5) Seatbelt violations

   Using seatbelts dramatically reduces the chance of injury or fatality in a motor vehicle incident. The NTHSA reports that seatbelts saved 14,955 lives in 2017. It is now NYS law that everyone riding in a motor vehicle—including backseat passengers of all ages—must wear their seatbelts appropriately

6) Cell phone violations

   Cell phones. Everyone has them. Everyone is distracted by them—especially in the wonderful world of driving. A cell phone violation in NYS will indeed result in a traffic ticket and 5 violation points against your driver's license

7) Sobriety checks

   Drunk driving has caused many fatalities in the United States. While it's pretty easy to spot a drunk driver on the road, the NHTSA (2022) reports that 28 people were killed per day in the United States by drunk driving; one person every 52 minutes.

8) Speculations

   Law enforcement officers don't give a reason for this kind of probable cause traffic stop. They are also less likely to take traffic actions. According to Mother's Against Drunk Driving (MADD), the average drunk driver has operated their vehicle "while drunk" at least 80 times and only 1% of drunk drivers are ever arrested (2022).

9) Multiple reasons

   These stops happen when drivers are caught in multiple infractions at the same time. This can include speeding without wearing a seatbelt, or using a cell phone while running through a red light. According to the NHTSA a person who is pulled over for more than one traffic violation is more likely be subject to a vehicle search or be arrested.

10) STOP signs violations
According to the NHTSA 7.3% of all traffic stops occur when a driver violates stop sign regulations. This is easily prevented by stopping when you need to stop.

The best way to avoid being pulled over by traffic enforcement workers is to keep your vehicle working and your driving record clean. Better yet, make a pledge to yourself that you will always follow the rules of the road and stay away from dangerous and/or illegal actions. Why? Because it's better to drive alive than have someone plan your funeral.

Move Over Law

It is a well-known fact that way too many law enforcement personnel and highway workers, simply trying to do their jobs, have been severely injured or killed, because of drivers who didn't think it was important to respect their safety or space.

How would you feel if your loved one never returned home from work because someone else wasn't paying attention to the road? It doesn't feel good to know that someone you care about was hurt, or killed, by a distracted, sleep deprived, or intoxicated driver. It feels even worse to know you are the reason someone else's loved one never goes home. I have heard many horrifying stories over the years from people who have been victimized by fatalities on the road. I've seen people have literal mental breakdowns in my classes as they've tried to cope with the trauma of loss, move forward, and regain their ability to drive.

The NYS Move Over Law was passed in 2010 to eliminate these unnecessary casualties on the road. Following the Move Over Law is fairly easy. All a driver needs to do is slow down and move over (if it's safe to do so), as they encounter emergency, public, and construction vehicles, zones, and workers.

People often ask me exactly what vehicles a driver needs to move over for. The answer is fairly common sense. Drivers on the road should slow down and move over when they see the following people and vehicles working on, and around, the road:

- Law-enforcement officials
- Police vehicles

- Emergency workers
- Firetrucks
- Ambulances
- Tow trucks
- Sanitation
- Maintenance crews
- Roadside construction

The consequences in NYS for failing to obey the Move Over Law are 2 violation points against your license and the following fines:

- $150 for a driver's first offense
- $300 for the second offense within 18 months
- $450 for a third offense within 18 months

Drivers also need to slow down for construction sites with orange cones. Many of these zones have posted temporary speed limits that must be obeyed to keep everyone safe. When drivers are navigating construction zones *without* a temporary posted limit, NYS law requires them to slow their vehicle down to a maximum of half of the normal posted speed limit. Drivers that fail to obey legal speed limits automatically have their license suspended, and are required to pay double the normal traffic ticket fines

My heart goes out to people who have been victimized by a fatality on the road. Driving alive means bringing your best to the road to keep yourself and others safe. Just as you turn your head to check for oncoming traffic EVERY time you see an on-ramp or try to make a turn, make sure you start slowing down and moving as soon as you see lights, vests, uniforms, cones, and/or reflectors. Please drive to *survive*. Follow the rules of the road and drive with a mission to arrive at your destination safely.

CHAPTER 10

THE PROBLEM WITH TEXTING

On April 7, 2012, two weeks prior to her 18th birthday, Liz Marks was driving when she got a text notification from her mom, Betty Shaw. In that moment, she took her eyes off the road to look—just for a second—and drove her car into the back of a flatbed truck. Liz nearly died that day, and in the years since has suffered severe and permanent after-effects—all because she got distracted by a text.

Since Liz and Betty's first video about their story aired, I've shared their videos with every 5-hour pre-licensing and 6-hour point and insurance reduction class I've taught. I highly recommend Betty's touching book, *One Simple Text: the Liz Marks story*. I often give out free copies to my driving students as a survival gift when they pass the NYS road test. After the Bible, this is one of my favorite books I have ever read. It is truly written as a B.I.B.L.E. (Basic Instruction Before Leaving Earth) that every driver should read to change their minds about ever texting and driving again. So, before we dive into the subject, I'd like to give a shout out to Betty and Liz. Thank you for sharing my goals when it comes to being safe behind the steering wheel. Your story saves lives, and I am grateful for all you've done.

The problem of on-road cell-phone use

One day, in Rochester, NY, I saw a man walking down Lyell Avenue with his attention glued to the phone in his hand. Around him, vehicles were coming and going according to the traffic light on the corner. The man was so engrossed in his phone he didn't notice that cross traffic had a green light before he walked into the road in front of an oncoming vehicle. He was hit immediately. The driver, shocked by what had happened, stopped to ask if the man was okay. Thankfully, the man wasn't hurt. He was, however, very angry. He jumped up and began to scream at the gentleman who had struck him

On another day in Rochester, I witnessed a young man riding his bicycle down Lake Avenue while texting on his phone. He lost control and fell off his bike, scraping himself up, risking severe injury, and sending his phone flying down the street. Both stories illustrate how quickly fun times on the phone can turn into property damage and serious injury.

It's true that people don't get hurt *every* time they use their phones irresponsibly. It's also true that every time a person uses their phone irresponsibly, they risk killing themselves and others. The other day, I witnessed a lady texting on her phone while pushing a baby carriage down a busy street. The thought that came to my mind was, "Wow, what a CPS child-protection agency moment." Why? Because that woman's irresponsible texting behavior was risking the safety of her infant child. Christmas 2020, I was driving home when I witnessed a gentleman talking on his cellphone while allowing his little 4-year-old son to cross a very busy street. The little boy was low to the ground in a motorized play car. It could have been almost impossible for drivers to see him. People forget that every year, children enter traffic and are killed in the time it takes for their caregivers to glance away and back again. It only takes a moment.

Even right now, as I'm sitting in the window writing this book, I can see a young man riding his four-wheeler in the rain while talking on his phone. I shudder to think what could happen to him if—*when*—he loses control. After all, it only takes a second.

In each of these situations, so-called responsible adults risked their lives *and the lives of others* by prioritizing screen-time over safety. As we aspire to Drive Alive, we must ALWAYS be mindful of our surroundings, including what's in front of us and what's behind.

Cell phone used and walking

Informed road users understand the dangers of phone use on the road and its consequences. This list of important statistics clearly illustrates why using cell phones on and around the road is everyone's problem.

Phone use and driving

"Under New York State law you cannot use a hand-held mobile telephone or portable electronic device while you drive. Illegal activity includes holding a portable electronic device and

- *talking on a handheld mobile telephone*
- *composing, sending, reading, accessing, browsing, transmitting, saving, or retrieving electronic data such as e-mail, text messages, or webpages*
- *viewing, taking, or transmitting images*
- *playing games"*

Drivers caught using their cell-phones illegally while driving are fined. They also receive 5 driver violation points against their license. The fines are as follows:

- $50-$200 for a first offence
- $50-250 for the second offense within 18 months
- $50-$450 for the third or subsequent offense in 18 months
- Surcharges will be applied up to $93 for each offense

Consequences are much harsher for drivers with a learner's permit, as well as probationary and junior drivers:

- First conviction = suspension of driver's license/permit for 120 days
- Second conviction within 6 months after license/permit is restored = revocation of license/permit for at least one year

According to a distracted driving study by the NHTSA[5], nearly 80% of accidents, and 65% of near-

---

[5] https://trafficsafety.ny.gov/distracted-driving-1, July 2023

accidents involved drivers glancing away from the road in front of them. According to the study:

- *"Looking away for two or more seconds will double the risk of a crash or near crash.*
- *Driver inattention due to drowsiness will increase the risk of a crash or near crash by at least four times.*
- *A driver who is engaged in a secondary task while driving also increases their risk factor.*
- *The following actions: talking, listening or dialing a hand-held device; inserting or retrieving a compact disc; operating a PDA; reading, applying makeup or eating will increase the driver risk factor of a crash or near crash by two to three times[6]"*

Committed to safety

What can we do to end this distracted walking and driving epidemic? The answers are simple:

- Pledge not to text and walk/drive

---

[6] Quoted from https://trafficsafety.ny.gov/distracted-driving-1, July 2023

- If the conversation is that important, find a safe space where you can take a break from driving/walking to focus on the phone
- Consider putting the phone away (or even leaving it at home) so you can enjoy the scenery

When we all work together, we all make sure that we can drive (and walk) alive.

PART III

REVIEW & APPLICATION

CHAPTER 11   TIME TO THINK

As I've mentioned before, this book is a basic guide to the ins-and-outs of driving. No book—no matter how complete the author has tried to be—is a substitute for the in-person expertise of a *qualified, certified* driving instructor. Note my emphasis on "qualified" and "certified." I recently had the chance to interview a lady who told me she took 50 driving lessons and didn't learn 1/4 of the things we've just covered in this book. Imagine all the things she needs to know that this book can't possibly cover. Those 50 driving lessons were a waste of her money and time, and they didn't get her any closer to her goal of Driving Alive.

Think "It's time to get a driving instructor"

All people can benefit from good professional driving instruction. Some people will need more lessons than others to fully form the skills and habits drivers need to be safe. This can become expensive if your driving instructor is more interested in racking up lessons than teaching you necessary skills. The best way to get the instruction you need and save money *in the long run* is to choose a reputable instructor/driving school. Good instructors teach efficiently by tailoring driving lessons to their students' needs. For example, at ABC School of Driving[7] where I work, we constantly evaluate our students. This allows us to figure out what skills need they need to strengthen in real time. While our prices per lesson may be higher than others in the area, we save time and money by focusing our lessons on our students' demonstrated needs.

If you don't have a certified driving instructor yet, use this book as a tool to help you evaluate different driving schools and instructors. I promise you that good instructors will emphasize all the content we've covered here, and more. As you move through your evaluation process, here are a few questions you might ask:

- Are your instructors certified? If so, by whom?
- How long have your instructors been teaching driving?
- Do you offer NYS driving courses, including the 5-hour pre licensing course and the 6-hour points reduction/education course?
- What are your NYS road test pass rates?

---

[7] abcschoolofdriving.com

- Where do you teach your lessons (on the road, on a course, or on a mix of both)?
- On average, how many lessons does it take for people to learn specific skills?
- What teaching styles do your instructors use?
- If I am having difficulty understanding/doing the material, how will your instructors help me work through the problem?
- What are your goals as driving instructors?

That last question is particularly important. The NYS road test is an important benchmark for getting your license, but it is only one day in a driver's life. Good certified driving instructors do more than teach than teach their students to pass the road test. They teach their students lifelong survival skills that keep them driving happy and healthy for decades.

Think about the road test

In NYS, drivers with learners' permits must always have a licensed driver aged 21+ in the car with them when they drive. This gives inexperienced drivers access to a more experienced driving perspective. Ideally, this helps them make good choices and stay safe on the road. There comes a point, however, when student drivers feel that they have enough knowledge and experience to drive safely by themselves. If this is you, take the time to talk with your certified driving instructor. Have them honestly evaluate what you do and do not know so you can identify any weak points. For example:

- Can you remember the first thing that you learned on your first professional driving lesson? If not, why not?
- Did the person who taught you driving skills teach you correctly? Have you learned good steering and vehicle control?
- Can you brake properly?
- Have you learned to change lanes properly?
- Do you know what all the different lane markings mean, and how to handle them?
- Did your teacher make sure you have experience navigating areas with multiple intersections? Back roads/ country roads? Multiple lanes? Toll booths? One way traffic lanes? Complicated parking garages? Heavy traffic? Construction? Etc.?

- Were you taught how to parking on uphill and downhill slopes? How comfortable are you with proper backing up technique?
- Can you perform parallel park and 3-point turn maneuvers in the right way, within the right time?

The best way to ensure that you're ready for your road test is to ask your certified driving instructor if you're ready, and for them to pre-evaluate you. Your driving instructor will catch any driving weaknesses you may have. They will then recommend a plan of action so you can be ready when your road test day arrives.

Think about life after the road test

Quick question: after you've earned the privilege to drive (hello, drivers' license!), how do you maintain that privilege? You maintain the good habits you've developed in your driving lessons and practice. You also make sure you avoid the following "don'ts" every time you step behind a wheel:
- Don't let yourself get lazy and develop bad driving habits
- Don't drink and drive

- Don't speed
- Don't drive tired
- Don't drive under the influence of legal or illegal chemical substances
- Don't have more passengers than there are seat belts in your car
- Don't drive recklessly
- Don't encourage yourself to drive recklessly by waiting until the last minute to leave for an appointment
- Don't take your eyes off the road for any reason
- Don't run red lights
- Don't drive distracted
    - Don't eat and drive. Seriously, that sandwich is distracting
    - Don't play with the radio
    - Don't live stream and/or use social media while driving
    - Don't play video games
    - Don't browse websites or email while driving
- Don't break traffic laws
    - Don't accumulate 3 or more violations in less than 18 months

- - Don't weave in and out of traffic
  - Don't cut people off
  - Don't follow the examples of unsafe drivers
- Don't drive when you can't see where your car is or where it's going
  - Don't drive with illegal window tint (they block your visibility)
  - Don't have objects inside your vehicle blocking your view through your car windows
  - Don't hang items from your rear-view mirror

    Don't rely on the mirrors to show you everything that you will need to see
- Don't stop checking your blind spots
- Don't drive children without car seats
  - NYS law requires all children below the age of 8 to be in a car seat while driving
  - Children under 2 must be in a rear-facing car seat
  - Children under 4 must be in a child safety seat. These often have their own five-point harness system

- Children from 4 to 8 must ride in child restraint systems, including booster seats and approved harness systems
- Don't drive pets without restraint systems
- Don't let animals or human passengers hang their faces, feet, and/or other body parts out the window while you're driving
- Don't forget the things that you learned to get your drivers' license
- Don't take the weight of your vehicle for granted
- Don't drive too fast to stay safe
- Don't drive fast where you see bridges that might have black ice
- Don't speed on blind curves

INSTRUCTOR REVIEWS

"Very good experience. My man Johnny Scott definitely came through and helped me get my license back. A very professional instructor. Thank you for the help."
---Brittany M.

"The driving school is awesome. They work with you closely. They are patient and they give you confidence you never thought you had when it comes to driving. I worked with Johnny Scott for my road test and it was a great experience…"
---Ikeda Jackson

"Thanks to ABC School of Driving and my driving instructor, Johnny Scott. He was very helpful and made it easy learning everything right and giving me a good time. I was able to pass my road test on my first time thanks to him."
---Edgar DeJesus

"I want to say thanks to Johnny. He really helped me to be confident about my road test and taught me some good pointers about driving."

---Anthony Lequear

"They were so friendly from the start. Johnny, my driver was very personable. He made the lesson as comfortable as possible, providing very valuable knowledge for the test. I passed my first attempt even in East Rochester, which if you ask me, is very tricky. WELL WORTH THE MONEY."

---Nigel Clark

"I am so happy that I picked ABC School of Driving. They were very nice and professional. A special thanks to my instructor Johnny Scott. He was an excellent instructor and made me feel very confident behind the wheel."

---Small Thoughts Décor & Design

"Had a great experience in the five-hour class. With Johnny's personality, it seemed like the five-hour class only took an hour. And the receptionist, Karen, was very attentive, kind and respectful. I also had Johnny for my pre-road test..."

---Duane Rush

"Johnny is full of personality and was fun to work with 😊"

---Gracie Hannah

www.ingramcontent.com/pod-product-compliance
Lightning Source LLC
LaVergne TN
LVHW050625090426
835512LV00007B/666